Scarlet E
(A Collection of Erotic Poetry)

Lois Glenn

Yellow Rose Books

Nederland, Texas

ISBN 978-1-932300-75-8

First Printing 2006

9 8 7 6 5 4 3 2 1

Cover design by Donna Pawlowski

Published by:

Regal Crest Enterprises, LLC
4700 Hwy 365, Ste A
PMB 210
Port Arthur, Texas 77642

Find us on the World Wide Web at
http://www.regalcrest.biz

Printed in the United States of America

Table of Contents:

Acknowledgments

Never ending gratitude to Cathy LeNoir, Publisher, Regal Crest Enterprises. She opened the door and welcomed a virtually unknown poet. Her courage knows no bounds.

Linda Lorenzo, Poetry Editor Extraordinaire, has my deepest gratitude for having the cunning to follow the broken chain of footsteps through the murky corridors of my mind while battling a swirling desert sandstorm. Linda is a truly dedicated and patient editor who created an instructive and enjoyable environment for us both to connect.

Many thanks to the entire Regal Crest Enterprises team who helped turn my dream to reality.

Sincere thanks to Marcy Glad for her insightful comments on my early drafts and the title suggestion.

My heartfelt gratitude goes to Cheri Rosenberg for your unending encouragement and unwavering friendship. Butterflies with multicolored wings may lead you on a path to secret things, but they still taste with their feet.

It is with great honor that I call Jo Gregson my friend. I'll gladly take a shortcut with you through a graveyard on a moonless night to rescue your wheelbarrow from a fire breathing dragon.

To my mom, Joyce Glenn, my love and appreciation for understanding that love is not synonymous with carbon copy. It is because of you and all you went through that I know I have never been unloved. There will always be room on my island for you.

Dedication

For the THUD-ders
You jerked me from the trance of dancing flames.

"Inside you cannot see me for I hide behind a mirror."
~Lois Glenn, *Shea's Eulogy*

Stepping Out

Just a Dance

It was just a dance.
Our bodies entwined,
swaying to the rhythmic grind,
twirling us away from defined reality,
rocking us toward our own immortality,
a magical force controlling our feet.
It was after all just a dance,
wasn't it?

Dancing Women

The grip of dance yearning
in the darkly lit room
strains against the soft
sound of the candlelight.

Settling into the rhythm,
a low gurgle of need
reflects on women who are
strong against the world.

Alert blue eyes ignite
within her sculpted beauty
feeling the flutter inside
of each escalating flame.

Tentative in the dark
awaiting the cue to taste,
all it would take
is one whispered spark.

Tender caresses explore
her measured score;
lips part in a lingering
hint of musical tempting.

The salty tang of her tongue
arouses the embracing flavors
of her deep shuddering moans
singing a musky crescendo.

Purring

Catching the twinkle in her gaze,
suddenly frozen in place,
I smiled and she winked,
setting the pending scene.

Leaning against the sink counter,
recognizing her gentle power,
sweet smells wafting from her skin,
my fingers entwined in silkiness.

Negotiating our first plea
stirred an undeniable heat,
opening passion's gate between
those strong legs clad in jeans.

Nice tight, muscled, and tall
spun around to face the wall,
leaning forward just a bit,
groaning in mock distress.

Covered in a sheen of salt,
desire reached its pinnacle.
deep inside a little voice
released a happy purring noise.

Lure

Visible in the cavernous space,
catlike coloring mesmerizes,
stirring the molten amber
of something deeper.

Semi-darkness illuminated
coffin-green eyes
existing to hypnotize —
memories seldom revisited.

Slippery inhibitions
removed from power
walk the few steps
across the bower.

Pent-up passions
beneath the wetness
hold her captive
with whispered reverence.

Golden Allure

Dancing sensually together,
pulsating rhythm casually mirrored,
fingerprints trailed down the center
in a mask of dark leather.

Waiting with intense anticipation
swept away by intricate sensation,
sliding stroke opens the shell,
sweet and ripe as a summer smell.

Subtle smoothness of molten touch
anxious to journey the wild elegance,
dark mass curls of warmth and passion
imprisoned with an invisible glance.

A heady carnival of aroma clicks,
composing a lesson in physics.
Happily, humming a tale of olden...
a stranger's allure is indeed golden.

Accentuated

Kneeling in the soil,
shutting out the world,
catching a glimpse of her loveliness,
illuminated by the desert radiance.

Eyes of blue flame,
forever untamed,
stared back unafraid
between the drawn drapes.

Beneath the folds of cloud cover,
round eyes glowing copper,
presented her passion
with a silent invitation.

The smell of her opening,
an exclusively treasured cavern,
cradled with tender caring,
accentuated their reaction.

Familiar Stranger

Feeling a gentle pressure,
she leaned against the stranger,
listening to her tingling flesh,
stirring familiar binding music.

Through the air the rhythm pounded.
Removing the last vestige of clothing,
her fingers trailed, ever so lightly,
mapping her steep hills and narrow valleys,
grinding against pleasure's sound,
clutching her restraining mouth,
sensitizing her entire soul to need,
begging for her raging release.

Helplessly bound and completely aroused,
sliding the zipper slowly down,
the heady mist of her desire
reverberated with her wanton cry.

Stranger's Embrace

Long moments of silence passed,
allowing the sun's warmth to caress
the side of my face, while I listened
to her comforting voice
melt the ice from my lips.

Aching to be held by someone, I sank
into her welcoming embrace
with a deep sigh of satisfaction.

I savored the taste of her mouth,
as I used this stranger's body
to comfort me.

Reality's Dream

In a solitary world of total self-reliance
I found pleasure in denying physical wants,
maintaining emotional control,
and refusing questions that had no answers.

I remained true to this obstinate route
until something unexpectedly stimulating
whipped me out of my reality
to ride a wave of desire's fantasy.

Feeling overwhelmingly frustrated
with a yearning for excitement,
I secretly wished to feed an appetite
that would shatter the silence of the night.

Edging close to the cliff
my hands fumbled with the jacket
when a light lick at the hollow of my neck
sailed me into a world of bliss.

Like the seduction of a huntress
calculating the distance
this sensual rhythm coaxed her prey
into an idyllic trance.

Sliding naked beneath the blanket
into the enticing fragrance of her scent,
the cloudy mirrors on the ceiling
caused a delicious tension to start building.

Caressing my nipples, tickling my thighs,
a passing cloud admired the sight
as the twinkle of twilight
thrashed in the sands of time.

With a candle's flame flavoring the air
our lips and tongues danced with flair,
sucking from forbidden fruits,
satisfying my lusty thirst.

Basking in the after-shock trembles
layers of silkiness upon my lips lingered,
as skeletal memories ripped through me like a blade
and my soul's window flooded with pain.

In a dark room reeking of mildew and mothballs
snores of absent friends filled the halls.
As dusty trees nuzzled a forgotten trail,
I closed the cover on another sappy fairytale.

Desperate to share the heat of loving arms,
my scarred courage, hidden just beneath a calm,
wiped away the hovering coldness
and stalked out of my calculated discipline.

Asked in a tormented sentence,
"Can fire cut through stone?"
The response came unwelcome,
"Only if you grow."

Revealed

Trembles drawing
velvety-soft sensations,
passion composes
unknown questions.

Answers spiraling from
warm moistness,
whispered benediction
breathed in a kiss.

Exposed lifeblood to
surging storm,
listen to pulsing
beneath a thundering rose.

Sparks smoothly ringing
the midnight bells,
tremor rising as sweet
torture deeply inhales.

Mere reflections of
experience and desire
tense and build
to exquisite fire.

Jolted into a single
moment of release,
stroking endearments
through wet heat.

Abandoned with grace
in animal delight,
heart's desire
exposed to sunlight.

Cupped Heat

Rocking Candles

Swirling blue water
revealing a star-filled sky,
spooned around each other,
shimmering from up high.

Breathing the mingled scent,
soft flickering warmth
finding a steady rhythm,
danced gracefully with the wind.

Floating small wax candles
pressed their mouths together,
trembling like a leaf,
blinded by need.

Mass of neglect
hidden in the corner
with a gentle finger
slithered out window.

Friction Bonfire

Deep slumber stirred in soft fragrant sheets,
wonderful world of visions and fantasies;
magnetic pull toward circular underneath.
Feel the heat movement would bring.

Hidden in a tiny concave,
trickles of arousal cascade
held and fondled gently,
igniting a sea of stormy need.

Caressingly sucked in rivulets,
flickering into hot stimulates.
Moaning fire of excitement,
never losing our silky contact.

Working in time with manipulation
pressure at a slow exhilaration,
sharp intake of breath ventured,
squeezing and releasing from pleasure.

Sweet honey perfume-shuddered escape.
Twilight lingered on strawberry nape.
Misty warmth nestled into an embrace,
tender moments gladly held in place.

On Fire

Arousal thudded persistently
crossing the open stable,
watching the smooth nipple
echo the heat building.

Burning in the window,
the throb of her throat
flushed a pale rose,
as our distance closed.

Tasting her kiss of silkiness
beneath the watery firmness.
Exploring this woman's secrets
captured in a sunlight mist.

Embracing her excitement
with yearning incandescent,
unable to resist
easing my lover's torment.

Tightropes of muscle grip
beneath ivory skin
as passion flows deeply
hot, moist and silvery.

Clutched in each other's grasp
tears glitter upon each lash.
Her massaging mouth between my legs
rekindles rhythmic flames.

Ardor

Desire twirled and swirled lazily.
Pleasure-hooded eyes sucked firmly.
Aching heat built precariously.
Inside pressure parted uncontrollably.

Passion saturated with molten questing,
Surge of engorging nipples pressing.
Tongue pulsed with unrestrained yearning.
Fisted tension hissed in tattered breathing.

Tilted softness of lips began exploring.
Faint pressure intensified in whispering.
Fierce passion throbbed frantically.
Slick folds groaned rhythmically.

Tenuous threads glimpsed surrendering.
Satisfied nerve answered the thundering.
Sound of pleasure tripped harsh and ragged,
So powerful and yet so truly inadequate.

Banked Flames

An expression wrapped in whispers,
eyes blazed with breathtaking gestures.
Endless chill absently buzzed,
thunder itching to combust.

Concealed inability to communicate,
gentle passion lurking to frustrate;
space between detachment and sensation
cocooned in murky confusion.

Under the halo of golden relaxation
peered overwhelming obsession.
Bridging the gap of consciousness and dreaming,
vague comfort prevents warmth from leaving.

Melted Together

Gently caressing her wetness,
lost in promising kisses,
enjoying the sensations
of my sensual exploration;

Worshiping her; hungrily
brushing the valley between;
drowning in smoky emerald,
accepting the gift she offered;

Licking all her sensitive spots
with a flickering tongue,
deeper into her passion
tasting with appreciation;

Sliding along her fragrant flow,
her body begging for more;
savoring her quaking flesh,
driving her to the edge;

Moaning in open pleasure,
hands tangling in silken hair,
clenching spasms wracking her —
steaming bodies melted together.

Temperatures Cooling

Spicy waves
shoot off sparks,
perfumed and shaven,
damp with expectation.

Single white clouds
lie in wait,
rigid with pleasure
like leaves in the wind.

Sweat-glistened stars
billow past lips,
blissfully, raining down
over every inch.

Thighs tightly grip
with labored breath,
drowning out every sound,
except her rising mound.

Rumbling earthquakes,
deeply contained
resonate pleasantly
with temperatures cooling.

Pleasure Wilt

Stroking her brunette tresses
casts down feelings of darkness.
Whispering arms cradle hips,
pulse point grazing lips.

Special connections teasing,
passion inferno arcing,
listening body opens legs,
gentle lapping of offered gains.

Reveling tongue increases sensation,
helplessly hindering vision,
pumping fingers inside
with cloudy blue eyes.

Shivers of incomparable pleasure,
heart struck deepest measure,
shower much-needed release,
limbs exquisitely wilting.

In the Glowing

Kneeling naked promise
in the muted radiance,
drinking in the fragrance,
pulsing with her essence.

Eyes bright as sapphires,
taking a ragged gulp of air,
not quite, touching her
musky scent of nectar.

Straining muscles
circle her dampness.
Puckered nipples
tingle with awareness.

Craving the supple sensuality,
magic fingers dip enticingly;
skin slick from exertion,
legs entwined in friction.

Breath slowly
relaxes its clamoring;
reclining contentedly
in the glowing.

Afterglow

Curious dancers
Walking barefoot through the stardust

Radiant smile
Slowly dipped into velvety softness

Pronounced pout
Ran fingers along the pool

Soaked fools
Lost in an uphill flow

Rapid soul
Settled over the dawning terrain

Moist center
Trembling in the peaceful flame

Nocturnal Hearts

Under the Sheets

Her flashing, rosy smile
reflected prisms of light.
Greedy and hungry for her
my teasing fingers quiver.

Laughing, dark eyes
spread her legs wide.
Wisps of dark hair
dancing under there.

With a quick glance
nails traced a path
along the barest accent,
a slow sensational torment.

Hips refused the bed
while pleasuring her depths.
Mouth tender, yet urgent,
sighed with fulfillment.

Blissful Sleep

Completely undressed,
teased into submission,
trembling in sweat.

A frenzy of rapturous greed
with each arch of pleasure
clutched the rumpled sheets.

Twisting from side to side,
insatiable bliss poured through
hoarse with incoherent cries.

Exhaustive surrendering delight,
slid into a dreamless sleep
in the deepest part of night.

Drifting Moonbeams

Tongues danced back and forth
playing a game of give and take.
Long fingers sank into golden hair
in recognized mutual pleasure.

Coaxing embers into raging flames
rewarded with sensation's taste.
Passions flare with ragged breaths.
Legs wrapped around muscled flesh.

Slickness on her trembling smile
arched into an unspoken request;
teetering on the edge,
unable to resist.

When the last spasm passed,
torn from gritted teeth,
soft kisses floated in gentle love
while moonbeams drifted, dreamily, above.

Pillow Talk

Braille-reading fingers create halos
along her skin's exquisite softness,
driven by some invisible steady pressure,
releasing focused eyes from the savored picture.

Earthy scent detailing passion,
bedroom sounds supporting expression,
tender souls surge in perfect rhythm,
tone turns to juice of silvery fiber.

Voice rolling in from the horizon;
echoing noise of seemingly random pattern,
thrusting moans around moisture
changed to gasping texture.

Heat quivering along inquisition,
after a misty speechless moment
straddled hips descended from the sky,
a protective gesture etched in a lullaby.

Whispery Sleep

Fighting against the wind,
dark clouds over the bay
crash against the shore.

Kneeling down before her,
naked on the muddy ground,
tongues wrestle for control.

Settling between her legs,
fingers slide into silky hair,
melting into her hungry kiss.

Glistening curls in the shadows
catch her screams of surrender,
drifting into a whispery sleep.

Lunar Entry

Crescent moon
inched forward,
grasping a long black curl
into a chaotic swirl.

Sunshine streaked
from her insides
beneath the aching stiffness
across her naked thighs.

Extending senses beyond experience,
bodies stormed with raging passion.
Coolness tickled pleasantly
below Earth's empty sheets.

Through thick tousled hair,
her spine puckered with care.
Pounding fluid detonated
tiny slivers of radiance.

My Dreams

Floating on the edge of sleep
caught in memory,
afraid of the feelings
just beyond reach
flickering, not steadying.

Shades of water and sky
darken the color of my
most recent nocturnal fright.
Afraid to open my eyes,
the reins of control untie.

Coming unbidden
a subtle sensation
of another presence
brings to me a deep
sense of welcome peace.

She is there in my dreams,
fiercely protecting me;
the stream of unexpected tears,
with her touch, slowly disappears
as my faith in us starts to clear.

Night Echo

Waves of unrestrained craving
exhaled slow and ragged;

Stretched a pointed tongue,
sampling the spongy region.

Hot, sweet and exploring,
the party was in full swing.

Surge of molten desire
screamed into the night.

Host of ebony stars
echoed in the dark.

Moonlight Passion

Overwhelming loveliness
fought for ascendancy,
strange obsession
almost rigid to touch.

Patient heart stroking,
silent encouragement spoken;
despite awkward position,
frozen in anticipation.

Dark soul, seemingly, empty
drove fear from the scene;
triumph of purest character
shining in the luminous desert.

Fire crackled across skin.
Kiss became molten.
Concentrating on sensations
made love of the branded.

Need beyond understanding,
writhing and shaking,
deep animalistic light
smiled into the night.

Magic Moon's Gel

Shimmering in the marble glow,
lips teased a nipple ring.
Confident of twilight's show
tongue snakes out, so slow.

Bare breasts pressed against leather
shook with suppressed need.
Voice pouring like rolling mist,
whispering her urgency.

Waiting lips pressed tight,
trembled in warm summer night.
Palpable aura of tension
turned into a throbbing sensation.

Deep breath licking her surface
added to heightened sensitivity,
shifting with signs of arousal,
drawing positive energy.

Tenuous threads of control
arched and bellowed.
Fisted hands in hair
pulling frantically at pleasure.

Fully blossomed red rose
kneeling in candlelit pose
wishing to inhale
magical moon's gel.

Marshmallow Shadows

Loot Mischief

Under daring skies,
teeth grabbed gently
her swollen folds between
raw desire's riptide.

Low growl surprised
her teasing set of nerves
with an exploratory dance
in a shuddering trance.

Slowly pressed,
determined to resist,
arousal clear and radiant
infraction warrants punishment.

The thin tongue of leather praise
swallowed with an unflinching gaze,
feeling the flesh open beneath,
disobedience sows what she reaps.

Primitive Pleasure

In an act of primitive pleasure
I bury my face in her cleavage,
smelling lightly of musk and leather,
and lick between her breasts, so tender.

Lush and ripe for the taking,
whispery strokes in velvet
joined by animal passion
push away all reason.

Bare skin ripples in the breeze
allowing desire's rage to unfold;
screaming in sheer ecstasy,
rejuvenating my weary soul.

Bound Passion

Dark turbulent eyes
with an angelic face
lying naked across the bed,
sexily draped on the pillows,
passion bound in compliance.

Relishing the scent of her vulnerability,
tongue roaming and caressing softly
breasts rising with hardened nipples.
Hands strong yet soothing
cupping the pale red triangle.

Devilish grin fondling swollen flesh
teasing with a burst of heat.
Sensation of desire touching every nerve
rocking against the restraints,
moaning into the incredible wetness.

Combined thrusts clutching the sheets
pulsing to the rhythm of thrashing hips;
ecstasy ripping through her body
with a throaty scream,
shuddering to unconsciousness.

Passion Beyond Pain

In the mist, coasting
sensation sharply centered,
not quite tasting.

Stirred in excitement,
moaning softly,
lost in the moment.

Dark triangle glistening,
ripe with readiness,
muscles pressing.

Overwhelmed by curiosity;
forced stillness,
waiting desperately.

Sinking into her mossy depth,
giving herself to this woman
searching for a hint.

Answers cast on leather
riding through the rain
toward a passion beyond pain.

Calling Out

Her wet center,
glowing in the lamplight,
a rare encounter of intimacy
spread out like a cloak beneath her.

Her fine silk of long hair
knelt between welcoming legs;
two fingers thrusting inside
curling into a fist.

Jingle of the handcuffs,
crazy with desire,
writhed beneath her
like a tropical storm.

A trail of blazing kisses
pushed deeper into
her increasing moans
calling out in orgasmic tones.

Triangle Fantasy

Lost in a steamy haze
three points of a triangle,
hot to the touch,
rotate between secret dreams.

Wild with hunger,
cherry-red gather
from the rhythmic mist
with anticipating radiance.

Deliberate movements
stroke their fevered flesh.
Flames of mounting desire
boil up from deep inside.

Scorched with a kiss,
a flickering candle
adorns their brilliance
as stars chase the moon.

Waves of rapture
crash their barriers,
breathless threesome
unimpeded by custom.

Gasping for Air

Expanse of flawless flesh
under the sexy robe
waiting for her caress,
feeling my wetness grow.

Wrapped in passionate embrace,
kissing softly...just a trace,
pushed against the wall,
inhibitions began to fall.

Handcuffs snapped around her wrists,
sudden feeling of nervousness,
passion-dark eyes kiss again,
melting fears to nothingness.

I slid down her naked body
spreading her legs tenderly,
and licked a hardened nipple
adorned with sensuous ripples.

Frustration pushed her upward,
closer to my waiting lips
With a very wanton growl,
her hunger pleaded out loud.

Delicately across her clit,
my tongue stroked the scented skin.
Her arching warmth met digits
and lips swollen from kisses.

Forgetting about the present
trust captured her completely.
Her body wet and glistening,
taking me deeper within.

Walls tightened around my fist,
moaning with each thrust,
sound of pure primal wish,
matching each penetrating shift.

Hair tickled against her knees,
my mind went blank, utterly;
blazing shudder of release
causing my breath to flee.

Not Foreplay

Circling slow
Iron hands
Mouth parted
Muscles grab

First penetration
Wanting it all
Pushed deeper
Making it last

Eyes closed
Murmuring faintly
Stirred and tightened
Surrendering distinctly

White passion
Fire ignited
Ultimate sensations
Cries united

Flipside

Gripping champagne pillow
among the roots of an oak,
bramble curtain displayed
prospect in a twilight patch.

Shadows stretch on the grass,
stroking the slippery walls,
ensuring muscled globes were slick,
allowing studded access.

Bundle of nerves touched
by a trapped ring wet from juices;
concentrating on the taste
while nuzzling the back of her neck.

Hidden music in the desert
increased in glistening tempo
muffled the moan that shook
and vibrated off the moonlit brook.

The Edge of Trust

Imagine the feel of smooth flesh
sliding softly across your face.
Darkness slowly lowers a veil,
first rush slightly concealed.

Sensuously circling appreciative shackles,
caressing strokes, embracing and primal.
Blood races, hot fisted in approval,
softened by the heat of leather arousal.

Unconsciously leaning against sweet chains
obvious offering of her binding pain;
private dance of consummate ritual,
dictated by the beat of mutual signals.

Intermittent glint of unyielding silver
catches up in the mystique of fierce pleasure.
Sharply sculpted features whisper demands,
cupping the flame of easy confidence.

Light caresses of a warm feather
blaze a trail down her quivering center.
Continues the onslaught until her wild cry grows,
the edge of trust defined by her echoes.

Guttural Surrender

In a suggestive way
an arousing bit of foreplay,
laced with lusty intent,
breathed in her musky scent.

With a tug on a nipple ring,
headboards started creaking.
Skittering over shivering spines
squirming sensations intertwined.

Something feathery rose
trembling with tender strokes,
increased the sensitive prompts
to strain in heightened bonds.

From her silky sweet lips pour
a willful message of wanting more
quivering touches with a hypnotic trace
of soothing warmth and a predator's grace.

Imagination and stimulation
dived into pools of correlation.
Unbridled carnal celebration
mounted in unbound exploration.

Emotions swirling in misty eyes
released mighty and soulful cries.
Lips moved to swallow her groan,
completely surrendered with a guttural moan.

Sensational Restrain

Heavy lids watching,
fingers explore lightly,
fire bursting in showers
against steel and leather.

Hips jerk in air,
struggling to focus
against the torments
containing her.

Whispering session,
pure desire's possession,
losing control rapidly,
need nearly blinding.

Breathing unevenly,
ready for release
her legs spread further,
the promise so near.

Thunder clawing.
Body sobbing.
She shudders
in orgasmic flutters.

Summer to Silver

One Summer Day

Sitting at the edge of a stream
birds settled into silence.
Hardly daring to breathe,
afraid she would vanish.

Agonizing feelings of indecision
disappeared in an instant
on a surge of white-hot
promise of fierce passion.

Waves crashed against the sand
fueled by an internal demand;
trees jumped within the earth
joining the love-filled concert.

A gentle breeze of pleasure
exploded into billowing silver
as feet dangle in cool water,
possessed by contented slumber.

Summer Nights

Summer nights feel empty
with storms brewing,
fumbling with a yearning.

Smelling the leather
blowing through the windows
a slow ache starts to hunger.

Balanced precariously on a pin,
needing to feel her supple lips
I invite my lover in.

Mouths find each other
slithering lower,
melding together.

She thrusts tantalizingly
with barely restrained urgency,
our bodies arched and blazing.

Deepening the moment,
completing our connection,
she tastes so succulent.

Shock waves bellow
as warm cream invokes
a soundless tear flow.

Tree Reflections

Lips through the leaves
whispered into the pool, beneath
hands planted upon the vast
rise of her lover's breasts.

Intense feelings of need
marked by the summer breeze.
Vice-like grip against her mound
unconsciously increased in sound.

Echo of rainbow water falling
coloring the fiery shade
excited by uncharacteristic daring.
Sun peeked through the maze.

Sunshine

Wet thighs wrapped around
rumbling chrome and leather
bounced without concern
along the rain washed ground.

Carried away on the wind
meandering explorations
rode the waves of passion
oblivious to the elements.

Liquid throbbing
conscious of her beauty
lost all grip on reality
with a muddy landing

Close to need,
this exquisite feeling
of molten arousal cream
bled through straining jeans.

Thunderous moisture
coaxed unbelievable pleasure
under the cloud covered stars
embracing the sunshine in her heart.

From Under a Cloud

An unspoken dream,
shadowed by dark circles,
tried to dislodge the cobwebs
reflected by slumping shoulders.

Her cocoon of privacy,
driven by need,
wandered the streets
seeking relief.

A shy smile
dropped to the grass
providing an invitation
to return her embrace.

Sensations in her silky depths
leaned into the caress,
willing to take a risk
for one stolen moment.

Love without reservation
rattled in the stillness,
taking possession of
her nervous lips.

A once isolated heart,
slowly surrendered,
with a cry of ecstasy
scattering her clouds of misery.

Misty Rain

Stood in the misty rain,
unaccountably breathless,
looked directly into her intense gaze
and felt an answering heated rush.

Despite initial alarm
abruptly began moving,
followed her confident stride
away from the crowded lights.

Electric wave of anticipation
smiled into the dim features,
too hungry to refuse
mystery of the ages.

Compelling hands began roaming,
buttons steadily opened.
Awash in hazy sensation
legs smoothly rocked in rhythm.

Head bending lower,
contacting with lips' warmth;
mouth's invitation answered,
spirits climbing higher.

Searching fingers pressing in
blazed across hot skin,
traveling along the curve of flesh,
doing enchanting things.

Sated roars of thunder
escaped with each gasp
as complete and utter surrender
pushed through the lurking past.

Silent Storm

Rain drizzled softly around
eyes warm and brown
reflected in the silent storm.

Music pulsated through the sea
waltzing in her creamy heat.
Breasts pushed forward, demandingly.

Lambent flames dance silently,
surrounding the cavernous opening
vibrating the muscles beneath.

Treading the edge of a pounding orgasm,
full lips enveloped the tender moistness,
surrendering in translucent rhythms.

Rain Dance

Hollow whispers of rain
reuniting in a tearful embrace,
soft music in the moon's silence
reflecting across a fragrant surface.

Flames flutter in damp warmth
tossing shadows back and forth,
painting flowers with a searing kiss,
petals dancing in the darkness.

Aromas sketched in blissful passion,
paused together in a sensual vision,
moments savored deep inside,
capturing embers without ties.

Bees blush in climactic scrutiny,
frozen in lushly layered intimacy,
roses dart across the window
blurring exposure's floating tango.

Surfacing from desire's shimmer,
relishing the scent of contented glitter,
entwined in sleep's tenderness,
drenched in avowed completeness.

Love Storm

One dark afternoon
walking in sweet dew
brushing against her mouth
sent a tornado through my house.

Spiders twist in the web,
swirled by gusts of wind
sparkle in the pale light
hunting through the night.

Lightning ripped across my body.
Rain lashed at the sheets.
Fingers captured for an instant,
breathing in her musky scent.

Feathers etched in shadow
circling a crystal rose;
red tinted leaves swirled,
stroking delicate curves.

Dancing between her fallen fences,
licking the hot tide of sweetness
churning her funnel deeper
drowning in her pleasure.

Breathing returns to normal,
fighting nature's control
pressed against her silken warmth
shown the strength of her love.

Crystal Rainbow

Alive with feelings,
a gentle smile
offered her kiss
under a crystal rainbow.

Teasing nips and strokes
spiced the air
with nervous tingles
flickering in the candlelight.

Drinking in her beauty,
satiny lips
tantalize the surface
with the image love created.

Fine mist of sweat
looked out the window,
hiding a grin
as darkness closed in.

Cracked Door

Notions

Feeling a little erratic,
past played its part
leading to suspect
sudden whims of the heart.

Sneaking suspicion
at the wall listens,
knuckles white with apprehension
blossomed to somber expression.

Still invisible in treachery
green stems swayed,
shifting under scrutiny,
clouding beautifully crafted clay.

Recalcitrant winds whipped up
a cleverly manipulated tension,
held on the brink among
physical and spiritual suspension.

While emotions are composing,
windows start clattering,
but steadfast in the glaring,
truth is completely un-tarnishing.

The Long Road

Gleaming in the morning sun,
her complete control
reverberated through the room,
growing in intensity,
sending a cloud of trust
and submission
racing through my body.

Covered in mud,
I melted into my lover's flesh,
lost in a passionate haze
not caring enough to stop;
one kiss at a time,
she continued to feast,
as silence nudged the door closed.

Whispered words mingled
with the stifling hot breeze
until the sun descended
behind the trees,
shutting out everything,
except the blatant signs
flooding my mind.

The eyes of a stranger,
old with knowledge
not gained from books,
brushed the cobwebs from my face,
shattering the fantasy
of this virtual embrace
into a dozen tinkling pieces.

Through watery vision,
I watched my stolen
emotional connection
stretch naked
along her back,
blurring the laughter
ringing in my ears.

Kneeling in the center
with the potential to be blind,
my eyes hidden behind
mirrored sunglasses,
I, finally, listened
to the voice
of my outrage.

Stripped of dignity,
my reflection stared
into the mirror,
lost in an emotional tug of war,
questioning her motives
while trudging down
the long road of recovery.

Stumble

Instant of filtered weakness
laughing at forgotten innocence,
sleep demons timed confusion
with an irony of suspended illusion.

Laced with a gentle gaze,
baited into cheap mind games,
as a curtain across her vision
lost the end of the sentence.

Clear hint of resentment
shielding tough moments,
anxiety twisted difficulty,
largest chain of uncertainty.

With a nod of farewell,
looked down and swallowed
trying to gather her wits,
moved completely into darkness.

Lips brushed sweetly
ready with a parting speech,
gave an answering laugh
not used to resistance.

Swiftly fading testimony
cramps balance and harmony;
crossed wires of a heart
vanished into the dark.

Emerald Confession

Flickering aroma of liberated illumination
immersed in passion and drenched in trepidation,
forging a bond and feeling the solitude,
gnawing swirls in the darkness of multitude.

Contrast between candlelit chambers,
a warm fireplace and atmospheric ember,
emitting majestic heat like a first kiss,
volcanic-release as misplaced patterns confess.

Secretly forced to endure this casual pain,
ancient stars uncover façades of a distant rain.
Wishing to inhale a passionate embrace,
sin revealed on a blazing green face.

Serenity instills as awareness floats,
scattering the flames of bewildered boats.
Tears turned to icy droplets on a marble moon
creating the vision of a rose in ebony bloom.

Hopeless Passion

Pressure developed
from anxious torment,
soft trembling
elicits gentle incandescence.

Crackling blazes quivering
across molten aura,
expectation mounting
from the caress of Pandora.

Paradox echoes
apprehension's conquest of reality.
Powers of resolve
entertain the touch of sensuality.

Cynical restraint surrenders
to fiery shadows of rapture.
Red gold fragrance
embraces a voluntary capture.

Love deepens the completion
beyond understanding;
conflict ascends to accept
kisses that are branding.

Control awakens
with whispered chimes of midnight.
Heat dissolves in
cascades of unrequited delight.

Disenchantment gasps
like one drowning,
endearments and curses
too numerous for counting.

Composed anticipation
withers with deceptive trust;
hopeless passion
lies shattered in bronze dust.

Trusted Deceit

Dripping venom from fangs so long,
silent echoes of a vigilant wolf song.
Truth's question shattered all around.
A silvery web, deceit's only sound.

With a heavy heart, you know it's true;
this siren's song beats only for you.
Icy chills laced with hope, so dim.
Step toward love, a chance too slim.

Acquire the trust of a hardy thief.
Ancient ruffians embrace the reef.
Even sharpened steel cannot defend
against blind passion's deadliest sin.

Stray Home

Submitting to the briefest pleasure,
lips gave themselves to wishful power.

Fresh from betrayal's shower,
red velvet wrapped around a fallen lover,
hollowed out like a whisper.

Through a break in the roadside brush,
fear sweats out from her touch.

Caught up in remembered thoughts,
nothing more than deep muddy ruts,
blue eyes lost in a stumbled rush.

Cracked in its patterned sunshine
beyond distraction and well defined,
a relationship that's distress outlined.

Unable to hold the words inside,
anguish escapes in a strangled cry.

Look at the bark, smooth and glossy,
hardened like concrete.

A breeze jangles the leaves;
knowing better than to admit weakness,
they cling tighter to the tree.

Infallible Descent

Her forest of thick night,
broken only by a smoky moon,
fragmented inside her crystal pool,
faintly, perceived the warm light.

Waiting in the cold cavern
A shining stone's conviction
prepared a special confession,
intended for the coming invitation.

My shaky smile faltered
above the grassy plains,
as unexpected rejection
stepped through a flickering haze.

A wicked smile raced through her body,
slamming shut the window of pleasure.
My emotional blender
shattered, echoing noisily.

Stranded in this rawness,
my eyes now choke on affection.
With discipline-hardened perception
I drift in naked contempt.

Possessive Gesture

Standing in the dim light,
her sparkling smile
splintered the silence
across the desert night.

Glistening in the rain,
cradling her lover's face,
hastily formulated suspicions
eclipsed her heart's intentions.

Jealousy twisted inside
the softness of her lips,
indisputable flow of denial
reaped the punishment.

Escape is not alternate
beneath a floral bouquet.
Her wounded soul remained
cracked with guarded decay.

Stray Nectar

With one smooth gesture,
her short silk robe
evaporated with anticipation,
disappearing from sight.

Ignoring the creak
of her soul's gate,
sheer desire dove in
to her pulsing heat.

Teasing the entrance,
drawn deeper inside
her cocooned sweetness,
the greatest blessing in life.

Passion-scented fingers
touched her lips
as a golden ring's droplet
sparkled with mirth.

Fleetingly, truthful silence
lit the solemn night
as disdain surrounded
the desert twilight.

Shattered

Standing at the edge of a moral abyss
A hunger I couldn't comprehend
Shrouded the tightness in my chest

Reeling from her tender kisses
Whispered against my heated skin
Allowing her to guide me onto the rumpled bed

Growing much more confident
I tasted the valley between her breasts
As blood rushed toward my throbbing clit

Lightning illuminated the misty mirror
Reflecting the stranger's muted tears
Sinking slowly onto a nearby chair

Walking into the moonless night
Refusing to put up a single fight
Dreams shattered in the flickering light

Handing Over the Reins

No Limits

Long hair smoothing
around uplifted flesh,
dangerous thrill skittering
over swollen breasts.

Hazel eyes teasing along
inside cleft
rhythmic contractions rising
with each breath.

Taut nipples echoed
within trembling lips,
kisses wrapped around
whimpering limbs.

Lightly ran tongue
through rushing crystal,
radiating touch
brought glowing pleasure.

Body convulsed
against soft warmth,
white light arched
inside silence.

Cries labored
behind dimmed vision,
heart shattered
all former limitations.

Surrender to the Darkness

Her mouth, begging to kiss,
gazed hungrily at black hair
expecting to spend the night.

Hands caressing her scent,
slipped between legs,
ripping her identity to shreds.

Feeling the excitement,
shivers through her body
danced in her fevered mind.

Twisting on scarlet ends,
the final memory of her soul
surrendered to the darkness.

Bone Deep

Pulse of building desire
peering over the edge,
hollow in the purple hours.

With a faint laugh of chastisement
supportive green, delicately, steps
over the trail of emptiness.

With no need to explain,
her subtle show of possessiveness
shook the dark thoughts away.

A series of heated kisses
pushes back the loneliness
filling my heart with devotion.

She had altered
the tickle in my heart
into bone deep emotion.

Exquisite

Silky scent of Shalimar
flowed from a satin shell,
a gentle kiss of arousal
containing an instinctive shiver.

Opening her offered eagerness,
fear brushed against urgency
reveling in the delicious texture,
demanding heat etched in memory.

Caught in a dizzying web of passion
with a spiraling sense of abandon
united in a dance of torturous attention,
half-hidden by shocks of dark sensation.

Sexual rhythm deepened the contact
mingling a jubilant spirit and pure love.
Consuming touch brought to the edge
cries of welcome pleasure, so exquisite.

Impact

Leaning forward in silence,
heat strongly generated together,
small kisses pulling the sky down
to roam with the dusty moon.

Swirling tongue consumed the desert
around the fingertip of restless desire.
Frigidity wavered like shadows,
revealed in orange and purple dyes.

Howling thunderheads reached the fields,
expecting sweet jams echoing rhythm.
Gray rocks sporadically launch flowers
flowing through granulated sea waves.

Inferno bubbled on unblemished flesh.
Molten craving delight increased.
Sparkling stars whispered absolute devotion.
Overwhelming sensuality rocked her emotions.

Coaxed Pinnacle

Sensations gripped
hard in anticipation,
breathing in scents
of growing expectation.

Sculpted butterfly
touch gently lowered.
Ribbons of moonlight
fluttered across creamy shoulders.

My questioning heart
echoed in her throat
as my tongue slowly entered
with an eager note.

Drawing velvety skin
along her inner cleft
with an arched desire
seducing doubt's theft.

Vision dimmed between
sensual embrace,
quickening stream
stretched rational space.

Brilliant wave of
white light flashed,
instinctive desire
echoed and thrashed.

Red-streaked clouds bringing
the purest of pleasures,
rhythmic contractions
entwining our savored treasures.

Hungrily meshed passions
denied rejection.
In wonder, warm picturesque
intensity cried.

Release

Caught with waiting need,
inhaling her powerful intimacy,
I drift outside the boundaries,
delighting in her feel.

Eyes shudder in offering,
collapsing on her muscled body,
not wanting to break the connection
enclosing my attention.

Full of excitement,
my guarded touch forgotten;
deep among my fingers,
anticipated satisfaction lingers.

Broken silence sweeps
with a wave of pleasure,
inspired cries answer,
clenching my release.

Plea

Mouth watering,
waiting to be touched.
Skin sizzled against me.

Demanding fingers
found glistening,
lost in rapture.

Point of pleasure
losing control,
desperate to orgasm,

Could only
whisper,
"Please."

Consumed Release

Illuminated by the fire
she knelt before her.
Eyes never breaking contact
she feasted upon her wetness.

Tongue explored her sweet warmth,
waves of pleasure flowed through.
Fingers weaved a trail up her torso,
her caress begging for entrance.

Flushed features
fueled by her unyielding hunger
gyrated against her touch,
locked in a passionate kiss.

Encouragement gripped the bed sheets
driving her over the edge quickly.
Screams of ecstasy devoured her
response with a strangled whimper.

Love Travels

Destined Flight

Wild passion sparks silky sweet delights.
Satiny fires tremble toward new heights.
Emerald and sapphire lock in anchoring light;
two quivering souls board love's destined flight.

Desire takes control; eyes turn inviting.
Apprehension vanishes out of lips, igniting.
Joined hearts surrender, equally exciting;
promises avow eternal uniting.

Impending dreams wrapped in golden splendor,
cerulean essence restored warm and tender.
Satiated calm descends gently all 'round;
enduring faith blankets love's echoing sound.

Departure Swayed

Lazy summer evenings
lost in past memories,
lie in silent ease
shooting the breeze.

Restlessness churned musky debate,
tracing outline of a moon escape.
Desire burning to invade,
body surrenders and thoughts fade.

Inhaling incredible pleasure scent,
smoky wonder skewered disappointment.
Voice filled with sensitive flesh,
moaned in responsive interest.

Purest expression of heart's companion,
washing over in honest passion.
Wave of newly found sensations
negated usual nomadic existence.

Drifting on the Wind

Betrayal sweeps in
with a broad broom
catapulting whispered
promises off a ledge.

Anger tumbles out of the shadows
baring each ebony memory,
as doubt climbs the ladder of my spine,
balanced like a gymnast on a leather strap.

Mashed in distracted
nerves and tension,
love staggers through
the chambers of my heart.

Veiled in swirls of mist
clinging to the mountainside,
a strip of silver sunlight
danced out of innocent eyes.

Hot velvet pulled me into a kiss
sending fear fed by insecurity,
like the scent of desert flowers,
drifting on the wind.

We Wait

Invitingly, the door opens.
A decisive step of determination made.
Pain dances in the heart's dismissal,
Captivation grants access.

Dubious steps forward taken.
Coldness penetrates the soul of a clicking lock.
An attempt to abandon the sequence made.
A repeat invitation solicited.

Breaths detained in a mutual pause.
The entrance stands unbidden.
Locked in a gaze of equal supplication,
Release or acceptance denied —

Unbending, we wait.

Tumbled Away

Glittering with a sprinkle of stars
and clouded with lust,
smoke drifted across
the face of consciousness.

Hugging the glossy night
sounds of pleasure
pale in the murky light
embrace each whisper.

Blazing with arousal
her subtle essence
dizzy against the railing
beckoned for more attention.

Stroked into a chamber
of secret silk colors,
shimmering memory yarns
tumbled away in the darkness.

Escape

Playful menace
in beams of golden light
gripped her firmly between
heated thighs.

Caught in the whirlpool
titillated with cold
swollen lips, soaked
need traveled through.

Sporadic gap in the mist
pressed against her apex,
riding out the raging tempest
bubbling with hot radiance.

Unbound fury pounding
on a wave cresting,
strangled moaning cries
escaped to dizzying heights.

Once, Long Ago

Hidden in thick clouds,
surrounded by solitude,
caution became my armor;
you came to me for the first time.

I will never forget
the honey in your voice
the confidence in your pose.

Desert night rushing through my hair,
there was an electric feel to the air;
a blazing fire that was fresh and true,
you had a tenderness I never knew.

Pausing the top of dark glasses
at the dip in my shirt,
your gaze was like a touch
trickling down my thighs.

Nimble fingers came into view,
heedless of my restraining hand
playing hard to get.

Stripping in a moving vehicle
leaving nothing to the imagination,
wreaking havoc with my mind.

The shimmering ball of fire,
tugging at my nipple,
sent the fear of discovery
disappearing into darkness.

Echoes of the wind
slid across swollen lips,
your seductive scent
rippled in the breeze.
Moisture beaded upon your breasts,
needing to quench this stirring thirst.

Fingers inched higher,
finding the throbbing ache
with experience and desire,
pelvis rising and falling
longing for your touch.

Long hair swayed
raking across hot coal,
fingers finding wetness,
legs turning to water.
Light from the highway
spilled over,
breaking all the rules.

Outside the window,
the mist is stealing in;
not a soul takes notice
when time stands still.

Looking up at the darkening sky
I sit watching the lights go by.
The night air offers no peace.

Seems like a forgotten dream;
once, long ago, on a dark road
love caressed my battered soul...

Journey's End

Unabashed fascination
breathing in a bottom lip,
stretched between open legs,
quickly took advantage.

Love deeper than harmony,
kissing her long isolated heart,
each warm touch of her tongue
released a jolt of appreciation.

Tight sculpted thighs
quaked with release.
Moist beautiful eyes
surrendered to perfect bliss.

In the quiet dimness,
unsure sights
helpless to deny
warmth and security.

Reality started edging in,
breath caught savoring;
every worry in her heart
stepped confidently to a halt.

Black-Edged Petals

Unrequited

I stood below her window
watching her ethereal glow
and dancing shadow.

With only the flavor of her spirit
and the touch of her silhouette,
my soul hummed with her mystical music.

A solitary candle splashing
colors of a fire echoing
over my empty reality.

Beneath her trembling surface
the resonation of a nauseous protuberance
pilfered all thoughts of a repeat performance.

My heart plunged to the depths
of impenetrable darkness
the night her flame vanished.

Widow's Parting

Laced with raspy calmness,
gleaming like fire in the shadows
stands an invisible barrier
covered in dust.

No one to share her sorrow,
no one to hold and comfort her...
walking wounded struggling
to keep the demons at bay.

Her spirit, remaining
unbowed even in death,
rushed down to enfold her.
For a moment her mask slipped.

Stroking the pale cheeks
willing to die for her;
in that tiny space of an instant,
hearts and souls linked.

Across the desert
a sliver of light zigzagged
along the horizon
melting her grief away.

Malignancy

Echoes of a shadow
proved her dreaded suspicion,
silencing her vigor
with endless nausea
and eternal torture.

One day her pains disappeared
with the thunder of tears
sweeping up the front stairs.
Now clumps of mowed grass
cling to all who pass.

Rainwater swirls as a reminder
over my bare feet;
beneath the cold surface
is no place for
life's triumphant defeat.

Last Performance

Anguish and frustration
flushed in connection.
Wind rustled tough exterior,
forced by abrupt departure.

Pain-shimmering tears,
body shuddered near.
Posed unbearable time apart,
fear tightened throat hard.

Despite the heat of the shadows,
moonlight peeked in the windows.
Fogged breath escaped
bandages of tattered remains.

Confused emotions pricked, jealously,
lost inside a crossroad fantasy.
Denial continued to haunt, until
rejected golden glow fell.

Lover's Gift

Beautiful lover,
faithful and true,
desirable in the darkness,
bristling at the circumstance.

Candle lit room embraces
affirmation of heart's place.
Familiar ghost by the fire
winking in firm espousal.

Purely personal moment
clustered with emotion.
Tears poured out
laden with smoke.

Intoxicated heart
weeded the herb garden,
stage of transition
sketched in blood.

Ash inches thick,
a gray haze of existence,
inherent power in a plea
manifesting in our reality.

Stalking her prey
sheltered from the sun,
her body, arousal-laced,
burned with amusement.

Death-fed kiss
shrouded in hunter's mist.
Eyes with longing
shared sustenance, vitally.

The stroking of her tongue
stripped her inhibitions,
burying herself completely
in her delectable feasting.

Senses tingling,
probed deep inside,
surrendering to the pull,
brought to newer heights.

Shuddering on the brink of orgasm,
pain cut through each spasm.
Waves of guilt shrieking
arched above the railing.

Desperate whisper
begged for mercy.
Afterglow of pleasure
grinned inanely.

Speechless with disbelief,
silence was commentary.
Grief-induced vision
conjured a haunted reflection.

Guarded identity searching
on leathery wings.
Small cave that would provide
a taste of a different kind.

Most precious splendor,
savoring the freedom flight
of an anxious predator,
shivered at her appetite.

Damp Silence

Licking the rain from my lips,
I looked into my lover's eyes,
aware of the battle raging within;
a sharp pang of longing and regret
knifed through my seasoned chest.

Under the sky's cloudy cover
staring down the barrel of a gun,
searching for hidden answers,
my mind echoed with the vastness
of a fantasy clinging to escape.

A shimmering rock of crystal sent
an earthquake ripping through my body;
sucking air of dust in great gulps
from the sea surrounding my heart,
without any audible signal.

Cradled in each other's arms,
two women lay in a slippery ring
of petals from a dead flower,
as satiny liquid slides over silken skin,
my soul waits in damp silence.

Skeletal Memories

Beneath the merciless desert sun
image of black-edged petals
walked into the graveyard
bathed in a mirror of sorrow.

Savored lovemaking shadows,
whispering sensuous memory,
passionate moments flooded her
soothing her soul's guilt and anger.

Gentle heart washed over her
enduring love behind skeletal eyes.
Molten fire searing along her spine
unleashed the cloaked images.

Slick bodies wriggled,
soaking up each other's aura,
through the starlit night
encased a sense of closeness.

Struggling in silence
truth struck the wall,
handed over the keys
wrecking the whole moment.

Worthless scattered bones
shimmering in confusion,
viciously slamming against
an empty patch of stone.

Dim light under the overhang
stared at the emptiness.
An eerie sense of resolution
closed the reminiscent layer.

Betrayal's Prey

Looking up at the stars,
holding a dozen roses
spread across her lap,
her broken heart
tried to find the path.

Cold wind ruffled her hair
encircling the silent leather
death of a love affair;
rain tracked her
mourning tears.

Incapable of living untrue,
crickets chirped through
the dusty underbrush,
pounding the horizon
with threads of her future.

Willing away all that hurt and shame,
betrayal finished the meal
dripping down her neck
and within a fraction of a second
made her lustful claim.

Tangling her hands in dark locks,
adjusting to the darkness,
moving about in the shadows,
a slayer must be tough,
indifferent to every touch.

Raking through the crowd,
her eyes anticipated
a hunt of a different sort,
the surge of excitement
meandered down her very core.

Unfolding like a flower
wedged deep into the sand,
reality had finally sunk in,
swirling a mountain of strength
with an explosive sigh of relief.

Love's Cemetery

Drowning in a pond
as silent as a stone,
shielded from the magic
heartbreak shimmering.

Afraid to knock,
grief curled into a ball;
snagged unruly locks
escaping in a spiral.

Failing to comprehend
the simple mystery,
bitterness knelt
at love's cemetery.

Facing Death

Broken fields of gravestones,
shrouded by flowers of gloom,
bask in the tranquil night
bathed in shimmering light.

Standing in the cemetery,
suspended in shadowed greenery,
wicked malice spied the path
like silver on a photograph.

Deep in thought,
a merciful warm glow
battled through grief's touch,
a treasure better than gold.

Shining in the dimness,
woven dark threads
quickly burned her core,
branding the lining of her soul.

Mountain Footsteps

Out of Seclusion

Hanging in the closet
welcoming the night frost;
a cozy enough place
to hear the sound restriction makes.

Tough folds of my fly
wedged between her thighs,
unlocking the door
to my hibernating soul.

My previously skilled
tongue slipped inside nervously,
rushing through her wetness
sending shivers along my skin.

Like a shimmering desert mirage,
reaching through the layers
I inhaled deeply of her scent,
feeling the wind begin to change.

Entangled in a sweaty jumble,
wavy hair swirling,
her magical kiss spinning me
as the world started tilting.

Sharp exhalation of breath
wrapped in leather,
landed in outstretched arms
as the sun warmed the earth.

Boots now wander through the crowd,
rocketing toward my goal;
on a new mission
to step out of seclusion.

Trust

Dark smudges of eroded passion
ensnared in anger and dejection
drowned in her blue depths,
died a thousand deaths.

Desultory cobwebs bounced
inside trepidation's refracted prisms;
as the smoke of awareness descended;
trust stopped, completely suspended.

Not equipped to handle the intensity,
defiance opened the door with daring.
Tears trickled against the night sky,
mere reflections of the moonlight.

Dusted color of courage refocused
on the beckoning velvet present.
When the ash settled after the fact,
second chances dispensed by the pack.

An intangible treasure of the core
captured with mesmerizing force,
painfully breaking down defenses—
only way to unrestrained happiness.

Without a Trace

Peering out the window
fascinated by desert snow,
remembering rejection's pain
invisible to the naked gaze.

Forcing down the nervous dread
while fluffy clouds float overhead,
mocking memories of cautiousness
replaced with fragile happiness.

Fingers trace familiar curves,
as my lips finally meet hers.
Tasting a hint of chocolate chips,
splashes of sunbeams filter in.

Tangled in love's fabric
treasuring her exquisite magic.
Melting into her embrace,
insecurity dissolves without a trace.

Argument

We drifted off to sleep
after angry lovemaking,
totally at the mercy
of mirrored dreams
permitted to journey
like cold rain.

Contained in a beautiful
old chest,
treasured memories
icy to the touch
waited patiently,
hungry for our embrace.

Surrounded in darkness,
emotion colored
her voice,
flooded with
visions crawling
across my tingling lips.

A warmed and gentle heart
emerged from the cave
in the golden hues
of the setting sun
dancing into deep
emerald pools.

Amidst the rubble,
long brown curls
cascaded down her back,
returning my doubts
to their murky crevices,
smiling in relief.

Flavor of a True Heart

Chocolate box of frozen landscape
burdened by loss and pain,
unable to resist her lover's plea
atop the shattered pillar's peak.

Words laced with venom
given the majority of attention,
streaming black fire dotted
every drop of burning blood.

Expected journey of a will
floods the white mug of integrity.
Fleecy jacket of moral courage
steadies the goal of destiny.

With confidence and affirmation
dealt in infinite scrutiny
descending into the dark,
only the flavor of a true heart.

Ebony Mirror

Waking up drenched in sweat,
trembling at the shadows,
on the edge of madness
the dark entangles me.

This blaze of doubt burns
with nighttime loneliness
drinking around my own
overwhelming terror.

In the distance,
across the feathered sand,
the spell of your voice
ripples over the treeless land.

Your body covers mine
like war paint,
guilt and panic
crumple in my fist.

Lifting like the mist,
a whisper of a kiss
cracks the ebony mirror,
releasing my tainted soul.

Connectedness

Mantle of longing
suffused in brightness;
errant ramblings
smoothes away edginess.

Steadfast heart
ricocheting loneliness,
irrepressible urges prey on
deep-rooted emptiness.

Suggestive solitude
left completely powerless,
allowing the rhythmic
pulse of rawness.

Unexpected answers
compel the restless
escalating passions
isolated from tenderness.

Eclipse the intensity
with unyielding sweetness,
stolen breath
calms expanding awareness.

Elusive hearts open
glistening with wetness,
delicate spirits
spiral in timelessness.

Simple Understanding

Dark hair carefully masked
a glimpse of some haunted past.
Raw, intense passion burrowed
naked beneath her broken core.

Gazing out at scattered rainbows,
trying to contain what she shouldn't consider,
bright flowers awash in rain scent
couldn't repair a promise rent.

Chin lifted in stubborn insistence
waking up the warm sweetness.
Stars wink across the surface,
a patch of sparkle against the darkness.

Releasing a tortured groan
letting her imagination roam,
her senses losing all control
feeling the twinkle of her soul.

Through clenched teeth
a blast of burning intensity
gasped as an erotic jolt
rumbled in, sensation soaked.

Surrendering in a cry of release
resting in her moonlit peace,
a small quiet descended
at her breath's soft caress.

Her face reflected in dawning wonder
as simple understanding filled her;
true faith in a woman's heart
can withstand the most venomous dart.

Mirage

Black leather and heavy boots
knelt in the misty woods
Eyes roved around the options
revealing her glistening passion.

Entangled in aching need
a rush of heat surged,
hands drifting
driving her crazy.

A whirlwind dropped from the sky
yanking off her shirt in the pale light.
Naked flesh met for the first time
lighting a match in a room full of dynamite.

Breasts danced against fingers,
bodies melting together,
finely chiseled muscles
slipped trembling into her depths.

Slanting sunlight shimmered on the pages,
the dream simply faded
in that lonely desert place
as life began again.

Forever

Fire patterns caress their bodies
as lips begin brushing softly,
writhing with the memory,
groaning in sheer ecstasy.

Letting her fingers glide
over a supple thigh,
spreading her legs wide,
inviting her deep inside.

Struggling with her inner demons
blue eyes shine with tears unshed,
betraying her rising passion
pulling free of isolation.

Emotions erupt in her
desperate for her lover's answer,
intensifying with each tongue flicker
her kiss replies, "Forever."

FORTHCOMING TITLES
from Yellow Rose Books

Solace: Book V of the Moon Island Series

by Jennifer Fulton

Rebel Monroe is a Californian yachtswoman sailing solo around the world. When her yacht—Solace—capsizes in a perfect storm near the Cook Islands group, she puts to sea in a lifeboat expecting she is not going to make it. Eventually she washes up half-dead on the shores of Moon Island, where she is found by ex-nun Althea Kennedy.

Althea, who entered a Poor Clare order at 20, has recently turned her back on religious life after a traumatic experience in Africa. Questioning both her faith and the church, she is on Moon Island recuperating from malaria and pondering her options.

Rebel, considered a hero by the island's owners, is invited to stay a while and she forms an unlikely friendship with Althea. When this blossoms into something more each woman must rethink her identity, her demons, and her life choices before she can find real happiness.

Coming May 2007

Family Values

by Vicki Stevenson

Devastated by the collapse of her long-term relationship, Alice Cruz decides to begin life anew. She moves to a small town, rents an apartment, and establishes a career in real estate. But when she tries to liquidate some of her investments for a down payment on a house, she discovers that she has been victimized by a con artist.

Local resident Tyler Sorensen has a track record of countless affairs without any emotional involvement. Known for her sexy good looks, easygoing kindness, and unique approach to problems, Tyler is asked by a mutual friend to figure out how Alice can recover her money.

While Tyler's elaborate plan progresses and members of her LGBT family work toward the solution, they discover that the con game involves more people and far higher stakes than they had imagined. As the family encounters unexpected obstacles, Tyler and Alice struggle with a growing emotional connection deeper than either woman has ever experienced.

Coming August 2007

OTHER YELLOW ROSE TITLES

You may also enjoy:

Lavender Secrets

by Sandra Barret

Emma LeVanteur has written off any chance of true love and is focused on her graduate thesis, when Nicole Davis, a beautiful British instructor, turns Emma's world upside down. Emma thinks she can finally break out of a comatose love-life, but when Nicole convinces Emma to help with her upcoming wedding, Emma's brief hope for romance seems lost. But is it?

Nicole Davis is marrying into a socialite family. But Emma's friendship pulls her in another direction, sending her tumbling into a world of undeniable longing. When Nicole can no longer silence her feelings for Emma, will she give up her picture-perfect future to gamble on a love she can barely comprehend, or will she stick with the life she's always known?

Set in New England, "Lavender Secrets" explores the boundaries that define love, lust, and friendship for Emma, Nicole, and the world they live in.

ISBN 978-1-932300-73-4

Butch Girls Can Fix Anything

by Paula Offutt

Kelly Walker can fix anything—except herself. Grace Owens seeks a stable community of friends for herself and her daughter. Lucy Owens wants help with her fourth-grade math. As their stories unfold in the fictional town of High Pond, N.C., each must deal with her own version of trust, risks, and what makes someone strong.

ISBN 978-1-932300-74-1

OTHER YELLOW ROSE PUBLICATIONS

Sandra Barret	Lavender Secrets	978-1-932300-73-4
Georgia Beers	Thy Neighbor's Wife	1-932300-15-5
Carrie Brennan	Curve	1-932300-41-4
Carrie Carr	Destiny's Bridge	1-932300-11-2
Carrie Carr	Faith's Crossing	1-932300-12-0
Carrie Carr	Hope's Path	1-932300-40-6
Carrie Carr	Love's Journey	1-930928-67-X
Carrie Carr	Strength of the Heart	1-930928-75-0
Carrie Carr	Something to Be Thankful For	1-932300-04-X
Carrie Carr	Diving Into the Turn	978-1-932300-54-3
Linda Crist	Galveston 1900: Swept Away	1-932300-44-9
Linda Crist	The Bluest Eyes in Texas	978-1-932300-48-2
Jennifer Fulton	Passion Bay	1-932300-25-2
Jennifer Fulton	Saving Grace	1-932300-26-0
Jennifer Fulton	The Sacred Shore	1-932300-35-X
Jennifer Fulton	A Guarded Heart	1-932300-37-6
Jennifer Fulton	Dark Dreamer	1-932300-46-5
Anna Furtado	The Heart's Desire	1-932300-32-5
Lois Glenn	Scarlet E	978-1-932300-75-8
Gabrielle Goldsby	The Caretaker's Daughter	1-932300-18-X
Melissa Good	Eye of the Storm	1-932300-13-9
Melissa Good	Thicker Than Water	1-932300-24-4
Melissa Good	Terrors of the High Seas	1-932300-45-7
Melissa Good	Tropical Storm	978-1-932300-60-4
Maya Indigal	Until Soon	1-932300-31-7
Lori L. Lake	Different Dress	1-932300-08-2
Lori L. Lake	Ricochet In Time	1-932300-17-1
K. E. Lane	And, Playing the Role of Herself	978-1-932300-72-7
J. Y Morgan	Learning To Trust	978-1-932300-59-8
A. K. Naten	Turning Tides	978-1-932300-47-5
Meghan O'Brien	Infinite Loop	1-932300-42-2
Paula Offutt	Butch Girls Can Fix Anything	978-1-932300-74-1
Sharon Smith	Into The Dark	1-932300-38-4
Surtees and Dunne	True Colours	978-1-932300-52-9
Surtees and Dunne	Many Roads to Travel	978-1-932300-55-0
Cate Swannell	Heart's Passage	1-932300-09-0
Cate Swannell	No Ocean Deep	1-932300-36-8
L. A. Tucker	The Light Fantastic	1-932300-14-7

About the Author:

Lois likes to build sand castles with quicksand, jump in and out of things, including moving vehicles, play with frogs, and walk through pits of angry rattlesnakes. Lois' poetry has been showcased at www.justaboutwrite.com.

Email Lois at loisglennpoet@aol.com or visit her website www.loisglenn.50megs.com.

VISIT US ONLINE AT

www.regalcrest.biz

At the Regal Crest Website You'll Find

- The latest news about forthcoming titles and new releases

- Our complete backlist of romance, mystery, thriller and adventure titles

- Information about your favorite authors

- Current bestsellers

Regal Crest titles are available from all progressive booksellers and online at StarCrossed Productions, (www.scp-inc.biz), or at www.amazon.com, www.bamm.com, www.barnesandnoble.com, and many others.

Printed in the United States
68836LVS00006B/346-357